Buddha In The [

Preface

Understanding ho... ... pain in the relationships we share. And now this relates to the Four Noble Truths.

Why understanding The Noble Eightfold Path is the recipe for a successful relationship.

How does practicing a conscious relationship help you reconnect intimately in the bedroom?

Buddha In The Bedroom Daily Practice.

By Mel Cooper
Copyright 2010 Mel Cooper

All rights reserved - Melissa Cooper
No part of this book may be reproduced or transmitted in may form or by any means, graphic, electronic or mechanical, including photocopying, recording, taping or by any information storage retrieval system, without the permission, in writing from the publisher.
www.melcooper.com.au

Buddha In The Bedroom
Online Course & Workbook

The Buddha in the Bedroom 12 Week Online Course will guide you through the process of reconnecting with your partner and will help you to rekindle the joy in your relationship. Visit www.melcooper.com.au to sign up.

Preface

For over 28 years I have been searching, looking for a place to rest my heart and call home. I have studied and practiced many religions or spiritual beliefs. Those include Buddhism, Hinduism, Theology, Philosophy and Christianity. Buddha In The Bedroom was written from the heart, through life practice and experience. At the age of 13, when I got hit by a car and temporarily flat lined, I decided there was more to this world than what was before me and I opened myself up to learning and understanding the world I lived in.

Parts of that journey lead me into a 28 year process of understanding myself and choosing to live a conscious life.

Part of my growth was to put into action all the learning and practices I had personally and professionally studied. And as a Relationship & Intimacy Specialist, that was the hardest practice of all.

Particularly in the relationships I shared.

So as my purpose is to help others end suffering and connect deeply to themselves and to the ones they love, Buddha In The Bedroom has been created.

Have I found peace in a loving relationship?

Well, some of my closest friends would say yes, but not without the learning and loving along the way. I know that living with joy in my relationship is a continual journey through life which is determined by the choices I make, and it means nothing if I am not prepared to practice what I preach. There is no greater journey than the one you take with your beloved.

I have found that you can master your career, you can master your money, and your family, but mastering your relationship is the hardest path you will travel.

We have created an illusion of what we believe a relationship should look like, and if it doesn't live up to what we believe it should be, then we let it go. We never get the opportunity to grow and evolve through our relationships so we wonder why we keep creating the same lessons in love. And they are tough lessons to learn over and over again. It's time to take off the one-sided glasses and see the truth.

Everything you have ever looked for is before you, it is within you, there is nothing that separates you from your partner, all you have to do is understand, learn and practice theses basic principles and you will experience the magic of what love can be. That which is beautiful.....

Why understanding the Four Noble Truths - Creates the Principles for life together.

The heart of Buddha's teachings lies in the Four Noble Truths, which explains the nature of suffering. Suffering is the appearance of anxiety, dissatisfaction, fear, anger, resentment, and sadness.

So, in order to explain the Four Noble Truths a little more, let's take a look at suffering, and how it is caused and how it can be overcome. In Buddha's teachings he describes suffering as Dukkha and that suffering is ever present in the lives we live. So if life means to suffer, then in all things we shall experience it. We experience suffering by the choices we make, so in order to understand the relationship you share, it is important to understand why you could suffer in it.

Relationships are never easy. They are the hardest area of your life to master successfully. Our partner is there to bring out the best and the worst in us. We have become so precious when it comes to relationships and more often than not, full of our own self-importance. The relationship becomes more about what we get from it rather than what can I give to it and this is part of the reason why so many fail.

Just as working is an act of service, family is an act of service, creating wealth is an act of service, the relationship you have is an act of service. The more awareness is given to any area of your life, the more successful it becomes. Success is not measured by what you have; it is measured by the peace that rests in your heart.

You can have it all, but if you are not content, then you are not sustaining a peaceful life, and you are living in a life of suffering.

It is important to understand how and why we create suffering and quite simply put, it is years and years of conditioning, and the unresolved baggage we carry with us everywhere. Our insecurities fuel our expectations and it is our expectations that create suffering.

Let's take a journey and share the beauty of Buddha in the Bedroom.

If Life means suffering

Life changes, nothing is permanent. Ever flowing in movement like the river to the sea, in and out, up and down. Through a belief that things will stay the same forever and wanting life to never change (because it feels so good), we are sure to create our own suffering, through thought, through action. In life it is inevitable that we will suffer physically, with pain, injury, sickness, tiredness and death. It is also inevitable that we will suffer at some point emotional pain, such as sadness, fear, anger and disappointment.

In life we also have the opposite of suffering, which is peace, comfort, joy and love. There is an underlining fear that life is never really complete or whole, because on an unconscious level we know it is impermanent. This means that in all our striving to find the things that we believe shall make us happy, are never fully realized or achieved. Because even when we find them, happiness is simply a moment that shall pass and we place so much expectation on that single moment that it will never be able to live up too. In this we have created suffering.

Suffering exists because you believe, expect and perceive that something or someone should be a certain way. Letting go of the illusion you have created in your mind that this is what love should look like is the first step to finding Buddha in the bedroom.

So how do you begin to create a relationship that sustains itself through awareness and ends suffering?

Let go of any illusion you've created, of how things should and shouldn't be. Letting go of the expectations you have placed on the relationship and your partner is the first big step to bringing in awareness. Often this is one of the most difficult to shift. Your partner will never live up to your expectation of them, therefore always disappointing you, hence suffering. The pain is coming from you, created by you, not someone else. You choose at that moment how you respond to that pain. If your emotion has been created through a sense of lack, then where do you feel the emptiness? I know for myself, that it could be the simplest of things. For example, me not feeling supported in the family constellation. We share a stepfamily, so this dynamic can be very stressful when blending time together. You have different family values and different discipline processes, so parenting someone else's child can create all kinds of frustrations. We both had to accept that our parenting styles were different and give each other the support we needed. To do this effectively, we had to let go of being right and look at ourselves closely and how our actions created pain for our partner, and then take responsibility for those actions and creating positive a change.

It is very hard to take the emotion out of the situation and accept that your partner is not criticizing you, but bringing awareness to the suffering, which enables you to move beyond its limitations and create peace.

Understanding and loving what is. If we are ready and willing, then we are definitely able to move beyond the illusion of what we have created and evolve knowing that in suffering, you shall find the path of acceptance and through the path of acceptance; you shall have awareness and create peace.

The Buddha in the Bedroom 12 Week Online Course will guide you through this process with clarity and will lead you towards a more peaceful relationship. Visit www.melcooper.com.au to learn more.

The Nature of Suffering is Attachment

In the acceptance that all life is impermanent, we can begin to understand our attachments to what life holds. We become so consumed by our wants, desires, pursuit of wealth, passion, prestige and popularity, that we find ourselves never satisfied and our insatiable appetite for more creates suffering. The reality is that no matter how much we gather and accumulate to justify what happiness feels like, the less chance we have to obtain peace and live in the truth of what happiness is.

It is our ignorance and belief that to be successful in life, you must obtain all of the things you desire. So if that were true, then I would ask the question, why are we still unsatisfied?

We are so busy chasing outcomes that we have forgotten how to live moment to moment. The irony of this is you will never achieve success the way you believe it should be, whilst you have an attachment to the outcome. You will only create more suffering for yourself holding the expectation, and all you are left with is a feeling of disappointment and separation.

Your relationship enables you to evolve, and we will continue to create suffering until we learn to move with the ebb and flow of life. At the core of any relationship breakdown is a sense of lack, and lack is suffering created by the belief that our partner should be and do what we expect them to, and if they do, it will make us happy. We are so attached to the outcome, and whilst we are attached to the outcome you will never satisfy what the ego believes.

"If he/she only did this, I would be happier". "If he/she had more money we'd be happier". I love my partner, but". There will always be something else for you to suffer in whilst you have an attachment to what it is you believe should be.

Let go of the attachments, the expectations

and the outcomes you believe will bring joy into your relationship, because whilst you have them, there will be no joy.

You are searching for the idea of who you believe you should be through the relationship you have with your partner.

They are not responsible for your happiness, you are. And they are not the reason for your suffering, you are.

We have become so precious in our thinking and full of self-importance, that when we begin to let down the veil of separation we have created, we begin to see the truth and the reality of what is. The suffering in your relationship will not cease, until you change the way you choose to see it. There is a lovely saying: "Let go and let God".

Step aside and let your relationship rest in the space of peace and allow it to breathe for a while. Endeavor to let go of your expectations and the attachments you have, stop trying to control outcomes, and you will experience a sense of stillness and calm which begins to radiate through your relationship and only then will you begin to breathe.

The End of Suffering is Attainable
The unraveling of suffering allows you to disconnect from the desire to cling to or form attachments to things. You can unravel your suffering by understanding the cause and removing it, freeing yourself from the illusion of worry, which will bring in the peaceful state of awareness known as Nirvana.

Walking the peaceful path in your relationship takes diligence and commitment and whilst your partner is showing you love physically and emotionally it is easy to do. But, it is very hard to sustain the peaceful path when your partner is showing you anger or disappointment. It's very hard to live in acceptance when there is suffering in the relationship. When we hold onto pain fueled by every expectation and insecurity we have, it is the perpetuating revolving door. When will it end?

The only reality in this moment is the end of your relationship. The suffering won't end until you have had enough of living with pain. Wouldn't it be wonderful if our partner made us laugh, listened, earned lots of money, ate the same food as us, liked everything you did, agreed with you all the time and always did what you asked? And there would be no opportunity for self-growth into our true nature without learning and understanding whom our partner is and who we are. Without the lessons we have no movement into our own self-realization, and as life is impermanent and ever changing, if you try to stop growth, then it is inevitable that you will live a life of suffering.

It is imperative in a relationship that you both learn to move with life. As life presents you both with opportunity for growth in the relationship, it is so important that you remove the emotion behind the gift of change and endeavor to embrace it with an understanding that change is always for your greater good. I know it is hard to see change as always a good thing, especially when it means the end of something we love. What makes life changes bearable is how you to choose to respond to it.

In order for your relationship to move forward on a peaceful path, remember to learn the art of detachment and stop fabricating ideas of how your relationship should be. Your relationship is only as you perceive it to be and the reality of your relationship is only what you both have created. Remember there are two people who maybe be seeing two different things, it doesn't mean that either one is right or wrong. It is important to open yourself up to the truth.

It is time to ask yourself these questions:
How am I being of service to this relationship

and my partner?
It is for our greater good?
Is the suffering & pain worth continuing with to strive for the outcome you seek?
What do you feel you can do to end the suffering in your relationship?
Intuitively you know your heart knows what to do. I believe it is time to get out of your head and stop the process of over analyzing and listen to your heart. Only then will you begin the journey toward a peaceful path. So many of us feel unsupported, unloved, not heard and not seen in a relationship. It is through the suffering we have created, that we build our walls of separation to avoid pain, yet in doing so, we create more. It is okay to be vulnerable; it is okay to step outside your comfort zone, as there you will experience personal growth. You see, you cannot evolve without the lessons. But it is when we refuse to see the lessons as gifts of change, and begin to react from an emotive place, that our response to what is showing up becomes destructive.

To open your heart and begin the journey towards a more peaceful relationship, join me for the Buddha In The Bedroom 12 Week Online Course. Visit www.melcooper.com.au for more information.

The Path to the end of Suffering

Relationships are uncomfortable and to say otherwise would be a lie. In all the loving gestures we could share with our partner, there really is no greater than that of acceptance. Acceptance of your own discomfort in the relationship, where you recognize your feelings and let go of the story you are so desperately trying to cling too.

Discomfort is an opportunity for growth, and when you can find the gift in suffering you will learn very quickly, that it is an opportunity for love.

So many of you begin to threaten your partners with consequences should they fail to be the person you need them to be rather than the person they are. You can only push so much before your partner pushes back.

The cessation of suffering is to make a conscious choice to take the middle path. The middle path rests between that of excessive self-indulgence and excessive restraint from life. Meaning that to take the path of self-indulgence is to immerse yourself in life's pleasures to the point where you have become so disconnected from reality that you continue to chase what you believe will make you happy. But it never will. To take the path of excessive restraint from life is to become celibate to life's magic, for when we restrain from living we close ourselves off to love.

At the end of the day, you can have all of life's successes, but without the one element of life we have been searching for all along, it becomes meaningless. That which is love.

The path to end suffering is finding a balance that rests in the middle way, where you stop trying to find the illusion of joy through your own self indulged ignorance and open your heart to the effects of suffering and how you have co-created the path of pain. Only then will pain begin to disappear and you will progress along the middle way, moving toward the cessation of suffering.

Life is a constant journey, where daily practice becomes an essential way of living and you realize that living a life of suffering is not living at all.

Why understanding The Noble Eightfold Path should become the recipe for a successful relationship.

In terms of outlining the Noble Eightfold Path, Buddha described them as the following:

Right View (means to see the truth)
Right Intention (is about mental self improvement)
Right Speech (means to speak with kindness)
Right Action (means to act with kindness)

Right Livelihood (means to live wholesomely)
Right Effort (means to act with willfulness)
Right Mindfulness (means to bring full awareness to all things)
Right Concentration (means maintain awareness to all things)
(Reference Thich Nhat Hanh - The Heart of Buddha's Teachings)

From the Buddhist viewpoint, your relationship is a great mirror into yourself, in which we discover who we are. The mirror can either be distorted or very clear. It is an opportunity to see ourselves openly and honestly, as we discover our strengths, our weaknesses, our positive and our negative. The mirror becomes our teacher, if we are prepared to look at ourselves.

Our natural tendency in a relationship is to see what we want to see not necessarily what the truth is. In a relationship you have two people who see two different things. The relationship is thrown off balance and we would rather escape than stay present moment to moment. It is important to remember as we move into the Noble Eightfold Path that your relationship is the path and the mirror is your teacher.

The Noble Eightfold Path shows the way to end suffering. It is a practical guideline to ethical and mental development with the goal of freeing the individual from attachments, leading to understanding the truth about you. These eight aspects of the path are not separate from one another, but in fact so interdependent of each other that practicing them daily only supports you both as you journey on through life together. This is not meant to be easy, but if put into practice will definitely make your life easier. And this is no quick fix either. As with every change of lifestyle it takes effort before we begin to see the rewards. If you are honest with yourself and your partner, then you are able to move beyond the emotionally charged feelings you experience, and you will have success. I encourage you and your partner to look beyond what you believe and open yourselves up to a new way of thinking when it comes to the relationship you share.

Buddha talks about practicing right view, which means to see and to understand things as they really are. It is an understanding that the thoughts we have, determine the actions we take. And it is in the choice to view your life in a certain way that will cause you to react from the right space (being positive) or the wrong space (being negative).

So how can taking the path of right view help you in your relationship?

Quite simply, when you decide to take the path of right view and incorporate this practice into your relationship, you are choosing to see and understand the reality of things as they truly are - not as you wish they could or should be. You instinctively know that looking at your relationship openly and honestly will support you in making right choices that are for the greater good of you both.

Viewing your relationship from judgment will only create suffering and is not the reality of what is happening in the dynamics - Negative view creates a negative reaction. Positive view creates a positive response.

Wisdom comes from knowing that in order to see the truth of what is happening in your relationship, you must first be willing to take off your glasses of false perception and have a long look at yourself in the mirror. For how you view your partner and your relationship is every aspect of yourself you have chosen not to accept. And until you accept and understand yourself and the relationship you share, you cannot begin to practice the path of right view.

And the way we view the world is a direct response to how we set our intentions for life. This brings me to the next teaching in the Noble Eightfold Path, being right intention. This is best described as a commitment to mental self-improvement.

In Buddha's teachings, he says that there are three types of right intentions being the intention of renunciation, which means resistance to the pull of desire; The intention of good will, meaning resistance to the pull of feelings of anger; The intention of harmlessness, meaning not to think or act with violence or aggressively, but to develop compassion;
(Reference Thich Nhat Hanh The Art of Mindful Living).
The synergy between the two paths when in balance will begin to unravel the beauty of the teachings. So the way we see things in the world or in our relationships, sets our intention for the choices we make. So another way to look at the relationship you share, is by choosing to look deeply into what you both have and only by acknowledging the areas you both need to change, can you set the intention to make those changes. For example - If you have feelings of anger toward each other or

you want your partner to be intimate with you, even when they are not wanting too - then your intention (which is expectation) is setting up a negative reaction, that is not in alignment with the relationship. When this happens your intention creates the suffering that you both will feel and could super charge your emotions causing you both to operate from a reactive space.

In order to re-program your thoughts you must let go of any belief of how you feel it should or shouldn't be. This is the expectation you have around a certain outcome. The outcome represents what you think your partner should or shouldn't do to make you happy. **So how do you do this?** There is a very simple question you can ask yourself. *"Where would I be without this belief?"* You would be **FREE**. So to give you an example: If I believe my partner should be more intimate with me and show me more affection and it is not something he is comfortable with, then this is obviously difficult for him to do. I am expecting him to give me something that he is uncomfortable showing. This will inevitably create suffering for me, where I will feel disappointment and rejection. It would be more beneficial for both of us to learn to communicate how the lack of intimacy is making us feel or get help from a professional so we can both move through it, and rather than loose the connection, create more joy and more love.

Also consider that when you practice right view (which is the way we see things); we automatically begin to move into practicing right intention. If your intention comes from the heart space and remains free from any negative emotional charge, then you will begin to practice the path of right intention without experiencing too many emotional loops that you have to jump through.

Like anything worthwhile, it takes time and effort and when you learn to understand your partner and the way they need to feel supported and loved in the relationship, you create a space where you both feel connected, with a deep appreciation for each other and what you share together.

Every relationship at some point will journey to the crossroads. At this point, it becomes important to take notice of what the relationship is trying to tell you. And view it as an opportunity for change. Growth is essential to the success of any relationship and your partner is there to bring out the best and worst in you. They are also there to show you the reflection in the mirror, meaning that, for every finger you point at your partner, you should be holding five back at yourself. Because, for all the reasons you judge them, you are seeing parts of yourself that you refuse to acknowledge and this can create large amounts of frustration, which will ultimately affect the way we speak to each other. This brings me to the next practice in the Noble Eightfold Path, right speech.

The importance of right speech in the context of Buddha's teachings is easy to understand. What we say to another can break a person's heart or it can be an expression of love. What we say to another can create enemies or life long friends; it can start at war or create peace.

Buddha explains right speech as follows; To abstain from speaking with deceit against another; To abstain from speaking slander against another; To abstain from a malicious tongue against another; To abstain from words that offend or hurt others; To abstain from idle chatter that lacks purpose or depth. *(Reference Jack Kornfield After the Ecstasy, Comes the Laundry).*

Communication is one of the main physical blocks in a relationship, where the way we speak to our partner will either encourage you both to connect, or tear you apart. Communication is the key that unlocks and frees the heart. We come into this world communicating, but over time and through the parental conditioning we forget how and become so fearful of speaking that we loose the connection to ourselves and our ability to speak from the heart with honesty and integrity. This gets confused with the internal pain and suffering we are feeling, so rather than speaking from love, we speak from fear.

How does this serve the relationship? Well it doesn't. Even though you are getting something from it, be it negative, it cannot sustain itself operating from fear; it will eventually wither and die.

From working with clients to my own personal experience, (and I am sure many of you can relate), the spoken word can cut like a knife and can do lasting damage, especially when you are on the receiving end of a partner who is verbally projecting their frustrations onto you.

If you or your partner were speaking openly from a space of love, you would be walking the path of right speech daily - but if you honestly look at your relationship dynamics, how many times do you get frustrated, angry and defensive and begin to project that verbally at your partner?   Probably a lot and most of the time you are unaware of what you are doing.

When our partner is speaking to us offensively, it is our natural response to shut down and close ourselves off emotionally and for most of us we will shut off physically too. This is when intimacy on every level begins to disappear and we begin to view our relationship as another chore.

When you begin to understand yourself and your partner, you will see that how you view the world sets your intentions (expectations) for the way you respond to your life with your partner. The choice to hold the space of love, understanding, compassion and kindness becomes the conscious choice to make. You begin to realize that communicating with right speech will always leave the heart open to receive intimately.

It is also important to remember that when

you speak from fear, which is controlled by the hurt we feel inside, you will only perpetuate suffering, particularly if you do not feel understood by your partner who finds it hard to show compassion and kindness. This makes it very easy for you to begin to behave in a way that can create more pain.

If you were to stop and consider all the baggage each one of us carries and all the unresolved hurt that has been shoved into the corners of those suitcases, into every relationship you have ever had, then it is no wonder that when our partner show us the unattractive side to their nature, we begin to feel the impact. The impact of past hurts and the impact of the current pain we are experiencing. At some point the pressure valve is going to pop and too often it is not just our speech that affects our partner, we begin to act out or behave in a way that is hurtful to the ones we love.

The way you behave or act out in life is a direct

reflection on you. If you are feeling loved, supported, understood, cared for, appreciated, trusted and respected, then you behave in those same ways with your beloved. But if you feel none of these things, then it would be very hard to practice the path of right action in the relationship.

Right action means to use the body as a natural expression of life. This is why it is so important to become aware of all we perceive, what we expect and say, because it determines how we respond to our lives. So if you have negative thoughts, you create a negative expression, and if you have positive thoughts, well, you create positive expression.

Right action is the daily practice of acting with kindness and compassion towards those we love. Where you choose to refrain from harming them in anyway.

There is a four-part process that happens within the relationship constellation when it begins to breakdown;

The Expectation Phase - is the beginning where you have become disconnected from each other, time poor, distracted, a lack of fun, loss of identity, always giving and not receiving, nothing you do feels that it is ever enough and nagging. Then comes;
The Denial Phase - where you will experience a lack of self worth, you begin to trade off or barter (I will do this for you, if you do this for me), you feel empty and you have nothing left to give, you begin to curse your partner, you have thoughts of leaving. Then comes; **The Blame Phase** -where you have begun to withhold intimately and you have emotionally shut down, you keep score, you are resentful, you may have flirted with the idea of someone else, you may become emotionally abusive and sometimes physically and you feel your partner owes you something. Then the final phase which is; **The Alone Phase** - where you feel helplessness, sometimes this can affect you physically with a

sense of feeling sick, you can feel the financial strain, you might feel depressed, you feel as if you are existing not living, you have completely disconnected from your partner and family, you feel scared and confused, lonely and sad.

Right now I am asking you, **how do you choose to be loved?**

When you hold the space of love with the intent to be of service to the relationship, then you will be living on the path of right action. Your intent is not to hurt, but to love and this can be even more difficult if your partner is expressing anger or frustration toward you. It is important to remember the core of all suffering and pain - your partner's anger is your blessing. It is an opportunity for you to stay present and hold the space of compassion, which is one of the greatest acts of service you can give to your relationship.

Ok, so I can feel your exasperation, because in

the reality of your partner's anger and frustration the last thing you are going to feel like doing is showing compassion. You must remember that there is no need to make your partner's issues yours. You will only create more suffering and there is no reason why both of you should have to suffer; you will only make it worse. Instead, practice non-attachment to being right and accept that your partner is experiencing pain and find a way to support them through it. Love what is and accept that no matter what you and your partner may be experiencing, you can change any situation by changing the way you perceive things, the way you react, the way you speak. This will determine how you choose to act and the way you live your life, which brings me to the practice of right livelihood.

The way you choose to live your life impacts on the ones you love. Choosing a life that serves for the greater good of your relationship and family, means that by choosing to live a wholesome path, you have decided to not do anything that endangers them. Every choice you make is relevant to how you feel. So if we make career choices that are honest, with integral paths then we serve our lives in a positive way. Rather than career choices that are a means to get rich quick, whether it is selling illicit products or violating another person in anyway.

Right livelihood also means to look after yourself, by honoring your body and those of your children, by making healthy choices with food and exercise. It also means to not abuse drugs or alcohol, or gamble away your livelihood. For when you honor and respect yourself, you do so for the ones you love. I know it is cliché, but when you love yourself respectfully then you feel love, and when you feel self-love, you have more to give to your relationship.

How can you be the best you can be for yourself and your partner if you don't choose the path of right livelihood?

Choosing the path of right livelihood, means you choose LIFE, and you really become a true manifestation of love. It becomes easier to live consciously as you practice the conscious path. You naturally learn to listen to your body, mind and spirit when making choices. And these choices are made with awareness, enabling and supporting you to live your life in a positive way that benefits you emotionally and physically.

Anything that impacts our body or mind in an unwholesome way will effect our physically and mental ability to live consciously. Our willpower disappears and we won't be able to sustain a way of life with a positive outcome.

Your ability to maintain a healthy lifestyle will be directly affected by the way you choose to live and your commitment to your relationship to grow together will be affected too. This is when Buddha spoke of right effort, which is an act of will and without a commitment to change, nothing is achieved. It becomes easy to create distractions that prevent the mind from focusing on creating a life free from emotional and physical suffering. Your mental awareness is the operating system behind right effort.

It is important to remember that your ability to hold mental awareness will enable you to maintain a wholesome state of mind. When we loose focus our commitment waivers and our will to act from the heart space is misguided by our lack of discipline, so we fall back into our old unhealthy thought patterns and behaviors that we have created for our life and our relationship. When we fall back into old thought patterns, we begin to lose hope and begin to see negativity surfacing again.

I feel like I am asking you to complete a mammoth task, that can sometimes seem unachievable, but the truth is, that relationships are only as hard as you make them. And whether you are ready to hear this or not, for every part of any pain you might be experiencing in the relationship or believe that your partner is the cause of, you need to stop and breathe and take a long look at your part in the pain. It is a hard truth to hear, when you are told that the pain you are feeling is yours and often your partner has no idea of what is wrong, or what they are doing to contribute to your suffering. The more effort you put into life, the more life rewards you. So it is fair to say, that the more effort you put into creating a conscious relationship, the more you will live in a true state of mental awareness allowing you to stay committed to your relationship with joy, kindness and love.

Everything that I have shared with you needs a little effort, but only with the effort can you both begin to see the magic of your relationship unfold into its natural state of love.

Your relationship should be a daily practice of service, just like brushing your teeth everyday. Practicing and living in a conscious relationship requires you both to make an ongoing commitment to each other and yourself, to be the best possible partner you could ever be. To choose a life of mindful living, you must choose to live daily in awareness of your partner and the relationship you share. Mindful living can be difficult to sustain without the commitment, but when you both move beyond your suffering and the ego has no hold, then mindfulness becomes easier to attain and sustain. When Buddha talks about the path of right of mindfulness, he teaches that it is the mental ability to see things as they are with clear conscious.

Usually, the thinking, which is the cognitive process, begins with an impression, which is bought about by perception, but the impression doesn't last. Instead you begin to conceptualize by sensing impressions and thoughts immediately.

We then begin to interpret them and relate to other life experiences, which go beyond the initial thought. The mind then starts to weave a story of perception, not necessarily reality. And because we are only half conscious of what is truth, life becomes obscured. Right mindfulness enables you to become aware of the process of conceptualization, so we can actively observe and control where our thoughts go. Buddha's account for this is the four foundations of mindfulness; contemplation ***of the body***, ***contemplation of feelings***, ***contemplation of the state of mind***, ***contemplation of the phenomena***. *(Reference Thich Nhat Hanh The Miracle of Mindfulness)*

Practicing the path of right mindfulness in your relationship is staying present, moment-by-moment, and everyday. Letting go of your story, means to stop hanging onto the perception of what you think something is or should be - stop re-writing the story over and over again, of what you believe is and isn't happening in the relationship and step into a feeling state of what the truth actually is.

Ask yourself - How do I truly feel? How does my body feel? Is it true? How do I know it's true? Where is my mind in this? Is it experiencing suffering? Or is it experiencing peace?

Are you able to see the truth clearly without the emotional charge of pain?

Letting go of the suffering which is the control, or the need to be right, ends pain and brings you into a state of conscious awareness where right mindfulness rests. It is easier to see that staying on track and practicing right mindfulness daily will free you from your emotional challenges and your relationship will hold a space of peace.

You will then begin to realize that there is no other choice to make except that, which is one of compassion and kindness. Because a relationship that holds the space of peace engages in a daily practice of love. When you engage in a daily practice of love, you always keep the doors open to a deep connected level of intimacy that moves beyond anything you've ever imagined. So how do you sustain all of this to create, live and sustain a conscious relationship? Practice, practice, practice and the ability to focus your attention to living a wholesome way of life consistently.

If you would like to explore the daily practice of love in even more depth, join me for the Buddha In The Bedroom 12 Week Online Course. Visit www.melcooper.com.au for more information.

Buddha refers to the natural ability to maintain awareness and concentration as the last in the Noble Eightfold Path as right concentration. This state is best described as one pointed mindfulness. This is where all of your emotional faculties are unified and balanced. Right concentration means to have wholesome concentration and wholesome actions. To practice right concentration you must practice full awareness in everyday life.

Right concentration is the final step in the Noble Eightfold Path. Where all the steps, if practiced, lead to the way of complete acceptance. So how would it feel to the live in complete acceptance, ending all suffering in your relationship? You would feel whole and in a peaceful state of being.

The blissful state of being - Being present in every moment, every thought, every action to live wholehearted in everyday life with mindfulness in everything you do. From the gestation of thought to the manifestation of action for the sole purpose of kindness, compassion and unconditional love, to serve your relationship, your partner and yourself in order to live selflessly.

It is not hard to achieve, as with everything it takes a commitment to change. In my daily practice as a therapist, the one common thread we all crave is to feel connected to another and a sense of belonging, that someone loves us, and accepts us unconditionally. It is not until we change the way we see our world and how we create pain and suffering through our own lack of self worth, that we begin to see the magic of these simple yet effective practices.

You will then discover that there is no other way to serve yourself and your relationship. You do not have to become a practicing Buddhist, and I am not asking you to change your spiritual beliefs. I am only suggesting that you open your heart to a new way of thinking and know that when you openly and honestly take responsibility for the role you play in your relationship, no matter how difficult it is, and you practice these simple yet effective life tools, then you will sustain your relationship to live together openly and intimately.

All these practices lead to the path of love - the path of love leads to a deeper connection with each other.

How does practicing a conscious relationship help you find your Buddha in the Bedroom.

When I decided to write the book, I looked at my practice as a results based therapist and how I help others reconnect to themselves and their beloved. And I realized that the work I do is very much about you being present with who you are and who you become and in our yearning for connection, how it is very easy to loose yourself trying to perfect someone to be, think and feel like you. Because that is the way you truly believe it should be. From the moment you meet each other, the illusion of love is created because you believe you are in love with the person before you. Love is a learnt language that takes time to manifest in the hearts of two people who are willing and open to share it together. And what you believe is love, is soon lost when the veil of reality falls down and the truth of your relationship becomes one full of expectation and not the euphoria you once felt.

It is hard to sustain a deep level of intimacy if you are not connecting with each other on every level physically and emotionally. Intimacy is not simply sex. Intimacy is the ability to see your partner and I mean really see them, all of them, openly in acceptance for who they are. Including the parts of them that do not give you joy. Intimacy is about loving unconditionally, whilst seeing them as they are.

At this moment you realize that nothing separates you from your partner, including those parts that don't give you joy, because you acknowledge those parts within yourself.

When you experience a conscious love, you experience the greatest love of all, that which is unconditional. For unconditional love has no pain, no suffering and there is nothing creating a barrier between you and your partner connecting deeply into each other. Touching, feeling, loving, are all natural progressions, that flow like the ebb of the ocean moving into one another, because there is nothing that gets in the way of you both giving and receiving love.

So many clients believe if they can be intimate with one another, then all their challenges will disappear. Yes, in essence there is truth to that, but not until you deal with all the insecurities that keep getting in the way of you both connecting.

Let's look at it another way.

When two people who love each other, come together to be deeply intimate with one another through love making, then in that moment you both should be able to completely surrender in acceptance. Meaning you let go of all inhibitions, insecurities and fears that prevent you both from feeling the depth of each other's love. But this can be difficult to achieve if you are feeling any kind of emotional pain toward your partner or the relationship you share.

So it makes sense to work at creating joy in your relationship with kindness and compassion. Nothing can be truly healed by sex alone. The intimacy you both crave is the connection you have from your heart center, it is an energy felt in every cell of your body that automatically removes the physical component to making love. When two people come together to create love, it is pure if there is nothing in the way from you emotionally giving to each other.

One of the questions I get asked a lot, is how do we have sacred sex, or create a sacred love. So let me dispel a myth. There a lot of you that would believe sex to be purely physical, but that is only one part. You see you need the heart (emotional) to make it sacred. It is the ying/yang of love making where the physical and the emotional connect and it that moment you are completely free of any thought, just simply immersed in the energy of love. For in the presence of love, there is no outcome, you both are bathed in the feelings of euphoric bliss. Or otherwise known to be drunk with love. But if the emotional is not free from internal suffering, then you simply have the physical aspect of sex, thus it becomes a means to relieve stress, and you are in pursuit of the physical sensation of orgasm, where only seeking the outcome of temporary relief is the goal.

Let me stress temporary. Intimacy should never be forced, nor should it be a tool to bargain with. Sex won't heal the wounded heart. Only love can.

When you learn to let go of chasing outcomes, or creating suffering in the relationship you will naturally move toward embracing a sacred love. You will see its beauty, because you will experience first hand the embodiment of love both physically and emotionally and you awaken to the true consciousness of love. Where you both support each other selflessly.

Then love moves beyond anything you have

ever experienced before. You are both committed to engaging in love daily to be of service to your partner and your relationship. You see, when you both are experiencing love from the relationship, then love is what you have to share. And when you have love to share you do so intimately.

Buddha In The Bedroom Daily Practice

The following are gentle reminders to encourage and support you both in bringing awareness into you creating the conscious relationship you both deserve to share.

Open yourself up to seeing the truth, not the perception or judgment of what you believe it is. Be clear with your thoughts, that they set the intention for good will and come from a space of love in all things.
Speak with an open heart free from suffering, knowing that from kindness and compassion comes understanding.
Act with kindness and compassion and know

that you are responsible for your actions, not your partner.

Honor the body, mind that you have been given and remember the choices you make affect those you love.

Be patient with yourself and your partner, for all good things need consistent effort, then comes the reward of love.

Choose to live mindfully everyday with selfless love, living with awareness for your partner physically and emotionally.

Be committed to change and stay open to being the best you can be for yourself and your beloved.

Remember to breathe.

I hope you find yourself and each other and connect deeply to the truth of what you have been searching for.

You see, you both have the capacity for the greatness of love, you only need the courage to open your heart and let go of what has been holding you back from receiving the one thing you have being longing for. That which is

LOVE!

And there is no place you would rather be.

The risk of not trying to work on your relationship is far greater than if you did nothing at all.

With Love

Mel Cooper
www.melcooper.com.au
info@melcooper.com.au

**Buddha In The Bedroom
Online Course & Workbook**

Are you ready to let go of the illusion of what love should be or should look like? Are you ready to take your relationship to a new level and let go of old expectations you may have placed on the relationship? The Buddha in the Bedroom 12 Week Online Course will guide you through the process of reconnecting with your partner and will help you to rekindle the joy in your relationship. Visit www.melcooper.com.au to sign up.

Made in the USA
San Bernardino, CA
30 January 2019